Alderney
A Second Selection

IN OLD PHOTOGRAPHS

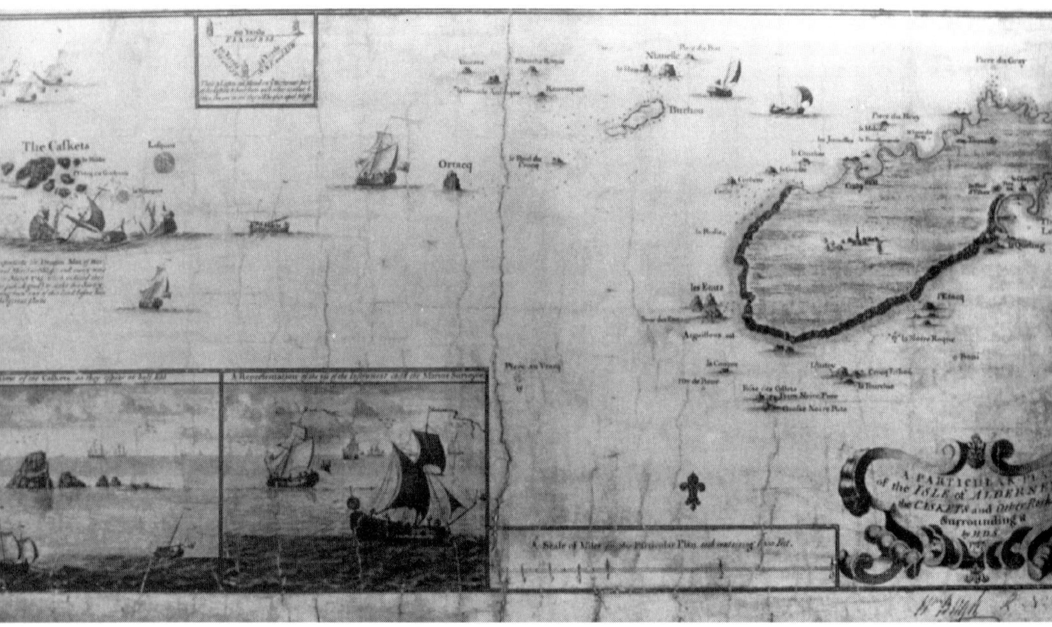

'A Particular Plan of the Isle of Alderney' by H.D. Sausmarez, 1727. This forms part of a complete survey of the islands made by Guernseyman de Sausmarez. Alderney is shown separately at a larger scale than the other islands. The inset at the top shows the layout of the newly erected 'Casket' Lights, and the wreck of HMS *Dragon* in 1711 is shown near the Casquets themselves.

Alderney
A Second Selection

IN OLD PHOTOGRAPHS

Collected by BRIAN BONNARD

Alan Sutton Publishing Limited
Phoenix Mill · Far Thrupp
Stroud · Gloucestershire

**British Library Cataloguing
in Publication Data**

Bonnard, Brian
Aldeney in Old Photographs
Second Selection
I. Title
942.343

ISBN 0-7509-0368-6

First published 1993

Typeset in 9/10 Sabon.
Typesetting and origination by
Alan Sutton Publishing Limited.
Printed in Great Britain by
Redwood Books, Trowbridge.

Copyright © Brian Bonnard 1993

For Jean

Contents

Introduction

The first selection of old photographs of the island of Alderney was especially well received by the people of Alderney to whom it was dedicated and, being launched in November, copies were sent to their friends and relatives all over the world for Christmas 1991. That production stimulated the offer of more prints from many people, including some from as far away as Chicago USA and Australia, and the demand for a second volume. The author is most grateful to all who have loaned their photographs for the present work, and to those who offered additional names for the people shown in many of the photographs in the first volume, and a few minor corrections to that work.

The photographs in this volume, most of which are published in a book for the first time, span a little over a century, from what must surely be the earliest photograph of the Casquets lighthouses still existing (above), taken by Jackson, of Jackson and Bean, the contractors, appointed in 1846 to build Alderney's massive breakwater. This appears to have been taken before 1854 when the height of the towers was raised by 30 feet to increase the range of the lights. It should be compared with the engraving signed M. Jackson, published in The *Illustrated London News* in 1868 and reproduced on page 100.

The people of Alderney are the most important part of its history, and many family groups and portraits are included here. The island itself and its offshore islets and rocks have a charm which attracts the tourist and makes most residents reluctant to leave it. The changing scenes round the coasts from hour to hour, let alone from season to season or year to year, are a constant delight to the senses. Naturalists of all sorts find a wealth of flowers, birds, insects and marine life, much of it unaffected by pollution or agricultural sprays and chemicals, with several species in each category at the northern limit of their natural range, and rare in or absent from England. The island has much to offer the walker who traverses the cliff paths, in scenic beauty and, when the weather is right, vistas of all the other Channel Islands and a large stretch of French coastline across The Race.

Quaint cobbled streets, most still with their old French names in use, and the majority of their houses well maintained either in the island's natural stone or in delicate colour washes, offer immense scope to the painter or photographer. The various fortifications, dating from several periods when invasion was feared, principally from France, during the many wars from Medieval, Elizabethan, Napoleonic, and Victorian times, whatever their present state of preservation or dilapidation, add greatly to the charm of many scenes.Workers building these unfortunately destroyed many of the prehistoric sites; nevertheless, much work was done during the Victorian era and more recently to investigate the remains of earlier occupation.

During the Second World War, when the island had been almost completely evacuated, fear of invasion from England to expel the German occupiers was the cause of the erection by slave labour of the vast number of reinforced concrete structures still to be found all over the island, many of them buried or part buried by almost fifty years growth of vegetation. Despite their evil significance these have also become part of the daily scene, and the most dominant, the fire control tower above Mannez Quarry, has long been known to the islanders as the 'Odeon' from its resemblance to some of the pre-war cinemas of that name. No photographic history of the island would be complete without illustrations of a number of these fortifications, spanning some 600 years of history.

The Victorian breakwater, commenced in 1847 when invasion was still feared, dominates the northern side of the island whether seen from land, sea, or air. Its construction, defence, and maintenance has given work in the island for almost a century and a half, and accounts for the introduction to the island of many of today's families, descended from construction workers and the military garrisons. The construction works also started Alderney's tourist industry.

The prosperity of the island and the size of its population have also been subject to almost regular fluctuation in connection with the needs for defence over the centuries, although many of today's buildings in St Anne date from the prosperity created by smuggling and privateering in the eighteenth and early nineteenth centuries, during the hereditary governorship of Alderney by the Le Mesurier family. They gave the island most of its present-day public buildings: Government House, rebuilt in 1763 (their earlier home, which subsequently became an hotel, then a convent, then the Convent School, then a German 'Soldiers' Home' and now, the Island Hall); the Old School (now the Alderney

Society Museum); the Clock Tower (all that remains of the old parish church which they extended several times); the present large and beautiful parish church (the 'Cathedral of the Channel Islands'); and the Old Pier by the Sea View Hotel at the harbour, built in 1736; all stem from their activities. They also built many of the old batteries and watchtowers for the defences, most of which were subsequently built over or enlarged in Victorian times.

Mouriaux House (1777), opposite the Island Hall, was the le Mesurier's later home, and most of the buildings in Braye Street, originally built as warehouses between 1736 and 1760, were theirs. The original building on the site of the Devereux House Hotel in Val Fontaine, and the Old Barn at Longis (now known as Essex Manor Restaurant), were parts of their home farm buildings, and the barn was later used as barracks, while the farmhouse became the Barrackmaster's House, and gave its name to the green lane leading from there to the sea. They also negotiated the erection of the first lights on the Casquets, which belonged to the le Cocq family. Starting from a petition to the Crown in 1709, the lease was finally granted in 1723, and the lights first lit in 1724, with armourer's forges kept alight at night by hand bellows in the three towers shown in the photograph above. By the time the photo was taken these fires had been replaced by a ring of eight Argand paraffin lamps in each tower.

Communications are an essential part of island existence. The two SS *Couriers* provided the principal link from 1876 until 1940, and again for a short time after the war. 'Big' *Courier* must be one of the most photographed ships ever used in the islands. Several other photographs of this vessel will be found in the first volume. The opening of the airport, the first commercial airport in the Channel Islands, in 1935, opened the island to further tourism, and air travel today provides our only commercial passenger route to either England or the other islands. The lack of regular and frequent sea links has also played a large part in the decline of agriculture in Alderney, and there are some nostalgic photographs of the agricultural scene as it was.

As before, my apologies for any inaccuracies, especially in the naming of people in the photographs or dates. Many islanders have contributed names to the captions to these pictures, but after a lapse of almost a century in some cases, memories are bound to fade, and few of the originals had names on them, so it has not proved possible to identify everyone in the older pictures. The author would be pleased to receive any additional information from readers in due course.

SECTION ONE

The People of Alderney

Formal portraits and family groups, some dating back to the 1860s, people at work and people at play; these are the essence of Alderney, and the items of greatest interest to many of the readers of this book.

The Assize Rolls of 1309 list the names of the two prévôts, the six jurés and the twelve men of the island or douzaine, who made up the Crown and Ecclesiastical Courts of the island. Eight of their twenty surnames could still be found in the 1990 Alderney telephone book. Most of the twenty names can also be found on tombstones in the graveyards on the Cotentin Peninsula, just across The Race, and some of their descendants still live there today.

Until the most recent influx of immigrants starting in the late 1950s and early '60s, few additions to the population had come from outside since the end of the Victorian building spree and the reduction of the garrison to a token force at the start of the First World War, withdrawing it altogether in 1929. A large section of the population was thus by then inter-related and many of the people depicted in the earlier of these groups are the common ancestors of several of the present island families.

Changes in economic circumstances on several occasions in the last two centuries have forced sections of the population to leave Alderney, and there are considerable numbers of relatives of island residents to be found in the former 'colonies', especially North America, Australia and New Zealand.

Today the population of just under 2,400 is made up almost equally of people whose parents were born in the island, and the families of post-war immigrants. Most of these are too recently come to be shown in these pages of old photographs, but today they make a significant contribution to the economic and administrative life of the island.

Thomas le Mesurier (1648–1718) and his wife Rachel de Sausmarez (d. 1685). The portraits by B. Graat of Amsterdam were done on their honeymoon about 1680. Thomas was a Guernseyman, first appointed Lieutenant Governor of Alderney on 31 March 1684 by Sir Edmund Andros, the 'Fee Farmer', who had bought the lease in 1682. He held the post until September 1690 and again from 1703 to 1714.

A wedding in Alderney about 1890. Elizabeth Audoire is in the back row, third from left, but can anyone identify the bride and groom?

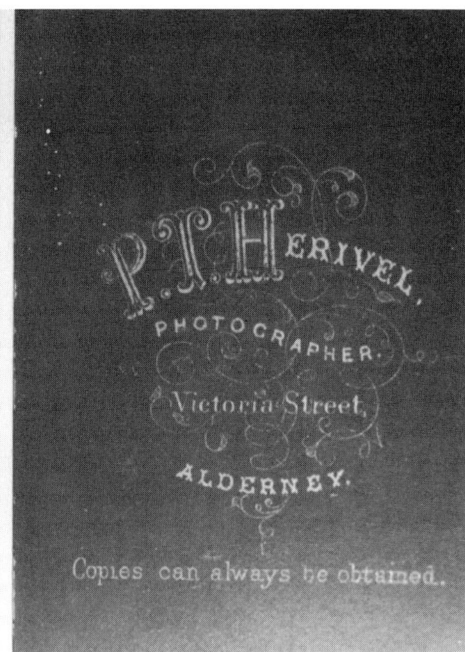

Two cabinet portraits by Alderney photographer P.T. Herivel about 1885. Only slightly reduced in size, the front and back of each is shown.

A family group about 1890. Left to right: Margaret Audoire, John Audoire, Elizabeth Audoire, John Charles Audoire, -?-, Tom Audoire, Florence Audoire.

An Odoire family group about 1947. Left to right, standing: -?-, Mrs Odoire senior, Archie Soffe, Helen Odoire, Teddy Odoire. Seated: Enid Tew, -?-, -?-, Kathleen Odoire. The babies have not been identified.

Mrs Langlois senior above Platte Saline in 1898. Her son, an Alderney Militia Officer, became Crown Receiver in Alderney in 1914 and held the post until after the Second World War.

Taken in Le Huret about 1910 this shows Thomas le Cocq senior, Grandma Martyn, and Violet le Cocq, née Martyn.

The Martyn family on Platte Saline about 1917. Back, left to right: Grandma Martyn, Edith Martyn. Centre: Liza Martyn, John le Cocq, Louie Martyn, -?-. Front: Bert ('Tot') le Cocq.

Probably the oldest photo in this volume, it shows baby Edmund Gaudion, born 19 October 1837, and his father.

Ellen and Tom Burland about 1896.

Mrs Margaret Benfield with Colin and Hartley
(in her lap) about 1910.

Colin, Hartley and Linda Benfield a little later.

The Featherstone family at Telegraph Bay from a postcard postmarked 1914. The Featherstones owned the Belle Vue Hotel at the time.

The voters in the Alderney courtroom are assembled to hear the States introduce the tobacco tax on 20 October 1919.

Mr and Mrs John Godfray junior outside the cottages at Quesnard about 1920. The eight back-to-back cottages were built by his father for quarry workers about 1850. They were demolished by the Germans during the Second World War.

The Burland family at Trois Vaux on 12 June 1932. Left to right: Thomas Wilkes Burland, George Wilkinson, William Angel, Elsie Burland, Ellen Louise Burland, Marion Burland, Mary Angel (née Burland), Ted Martel, Grace Angel.

Salvation Army Home League picnic outing, 1947.

RAOB Alderney Lodge about 1950. Left to right: Albert Rendell, John Dupont, Karl Curth, Fred Dupont, Jack Nadim, George Dupont, Charlie 'Mullo' Dupont, Barbie Cosheril, Nick Carré.

This family photo about 1935 shows left to right, back: Bert le Cocq, Queenie Regan, Kathleen Odoire (Soffe). Centre: Pearce Angel, Teddy Odoire, George Simon, Wilma le Cocq, Helen Odoire (Gough), Enid Odoire (Tew), Ruth Angel. Front: Fred Odoire junior, John Odoire.

A DH 86 of Jersey Airlines on the beach at St Ouen's Bay with Alderney supporters for the Muratti Vase football match, 1934. Left to right: A. Hanson, Jack Hammond, W. Barker, P. Catts, P.I.G. Simon, A. Després, Tim Allen, M. Jones, -?-, Babs Timson, -?-, George Jennings, G. Burness, R. Riou, -?-, F. Odoire.

Members of the le Pelley family from Les Videclins Farm, Castel, Guernsey, returning home on SS *Courier* after the 1935 Alderney Cattle Show. Back row, left to right: -?-, -?-, -?-, -?-, Miriam le Page, Elise le Pelley, Marie le Pelley, -?-, -?-, Tante Marie le Pelley, -?-. Rear: -?-, -?-, Mansell le Pelley, Annette le Pelley, Tom le Pelley, Don le Pelley, -?-.

Alderney Jurats, 1935. Left to right: A.C. Tourgis, C.H. Richards, W.H. Mignot, J.M. Rapson, D.S. le Cocq.

Alderney Wolf Cubs about 1950. Back row, left to right: -?-, Jimmy Cleal, Peter Gaudion, -?-, -?-, David Duplain, -?-. Front: Leslie Winke, -?-, Eddie Lihou, Danny Smith, Albert Randal, -?-.

1st Sunbeams of the Salvation Army about 1947. Back row, left to right: Capt. ?, Gwen Olliver, Pat Cleal, Mrs ?. Middle row: Esther Main, Nancy Jeffries, Veronica Cleal, Marjorie Millington, Vi Simon. Front row: Dawn Herivel, Nelma Petit, Rosalyn Blondin, Betty White, Jennifer Jeffries.

Judge F.G. French and Mrs French after his appointment in 1938.

Memorial to the Frenches in Norwich Cathedral.

Eileen Burke (Sykes) aged 6 months in 1927, with grandmother Elizabeth Burland (née Angel).

Cartoon from the *Alderney Times* in 1947, by its publisher Ian Glasgow. This shows the traditional testing of the Alderney fire engine in Marais Square on New Year's Day before the war. The engine, built in 1859, is still in working order after being restored in 1975.

Cartoon by Victor Prout of Alderney's first uniformed policeman Tom Lihou. The scene is by the old windmill at La Hêche in the late 1890s.

Wilma le Cocq (now Bragg), Alderney's first airport manager, in her Jersey Airlines uniform in 1936.

The Burland family on 13 September 1927. Left to right: John Bott, Marion Burland, Lilian Burke (née Burland), -?-, John Burke, Eileen Burke (Sykes), Thomas James Burland.

Four generations of a family together about 1937. Left to right: Rachel Rots, Mildred Raymond (née le Cocq), Royston Raymond, Alice le Cocq.

Some of the football players in Guernsey for a Muratti Vase match in the late 1930s. Back row, left to right: Sid Simon, Kenneth Allsop, ? Brown (Guernsey), Stanley Simon (Guernsey). Front row: Geoff Sumner, Walter Cauvain, John Knight (Guernsey).

Taken about 1946, this photo shows, left to right, Nellie Coombes who died in 1991 aged 104, Donald Coombes, young Doris Burland, Joe Burland, Doris Burland.

Taken a few days before the evacuation in June 1940, this photograph of the Salvation Army Band shows Lt Mrs Griffiths leading on the right.

The Easter ecumenical procession in Victoria Street in the late 1970s. Left to right from the front, Revd Ed Bennett (Vicar), Paul Crombie, Buster Hammond, Fr Henry Bradley (RC), Canon Bagot.

Boy Scout Freddy White in La Brecque about 1938.

Taxi in Le Huret, 1940, with Freddy 'Bibby' White and Mrs Harriette Simon.

'A good morning's sport in Alderney' by C.R. le Cocq, about 1910. The catch consisted of thirteen grey mullet and one blue bream, and totalled 66lb 1oz.

Balmoral Hotel and staff from the 1922 tourist guide.

The Catholic football team just after the war. Back row, left to right: -?-, Tommy Sebire, Bobby White, -?-, Bertie Cosheril, Bill Jones, Michael Mapp, Edwin Sebire, Danny Bott. Front row: Gordon Sebire, George Bohan, -?-, David Clarke, George Dupont.

Alderney football team in Barfleur in the 1950s. Left to right: Midge Dupont, Bobby White, Bert Millington, Bill Birmingham, Harry Mesney, John Bohan, John Millington, Buster Hammond, Ken Ducquemin, Peter Moore, Walter Cauvain, -?-.

The chorus line of Joan Holman, Lilian Odoire, Valerie Holman, Nancy Collenette, Jeanette Le Poullain and ? Pelzard.

A WI Christmas party. Back row, left to right: Maisie Allen, Mabel Rowe(?), Flo Riou, Alice Bohan, Iris Gaudion, Dolly Dupont, Eileen Sykes, Annie Shade, Christine Duplain, Mary Butler. Centre row: Phyll Catts, Elsie Cauvain, Cath Bickerton (President), Gladys Jennings, Minnie Simon. Front row: Edie Gaudion, Doris Curth, Mrs Birbeck, Mrs Easter, Vi Dupont, Gwen Rennel, Mrs Johns.

Young Violet Simon with a German gun on the Giffoine, 1946/7.

The Radice family in 1948. Left to right: -?-, Francis Radice, Julia Radice, Peter Radice, Sarah Radice, Bert le Cocq.

The 'Prix d'Honneur' float during Alderney Week, 1948. Left to right: Vi Simon (Dupont), Patsy Timson (Martel), Danny Simon, Lynn Sebire, June Clay, Fleur Riou.

The bar of the Harbour Lights Hotel in 1949, with landlord Bill Corbeth and his wife Molly.

Alderney Electricity directors and staff, about 1950. Back row, left to right: Bert Bohan, John Walters, -?-, Bill Mitchell, Billy Bohan, Arthur Gates (Company Secretary), Nelson Eaves, Jack White, Tommy Waller, John Berry, Bill MacKenzie. Front row: Francis le Poullain, Louis Dupont, Tommy Bond, Billy Benfield, Colin Fisher, -?-.

Jurats of the Alderney Court, about 1950. Left to right: Ronnie Hoskins, Ruth Herivel, Gordon Golding, Fred Marriette, Mrs Herivel (wife of Alderney's President), Home Office official and wife, Francis Impey, Home Office official, Charles Richards senior, Fred Odoire, Catherine Bickerton, Peter Radice (Clerk of Court).

Election night 1952, outside the Campania Inn. Left to right: Cdr Sydney (Toby) Herível, just re-elected President, Drew McQueen, Billy Shade, Eileen Sykes.

President 'Toby' Herivel and Clerk of the Court and States Peter Radice outside the Court House, 1950.

Alderney Week, 1958. Miss Alderney (Ursula Jennings) held up at gunpoint by Sid Simon.

Coronation Day, 1953. David le Cocq and Michael Lillington.

Alderney Week, 1953. Wilma Bragg with the 'Agricultural' float.

Alderney Week, 1958. Sid Simon sits in front of the 'Buggins Family' float. Left to right in vehicle: Mrs Phyllis Richards, Jean Richards, John Richards, Mrs ? Gaudion, Chris Gaudion, Bert Herivel.

Alderney 'extras' for the filming of *The Crest of the Wave* in 1954. Back row, left to right: Billy le Poullain, David Bell, Mike Burnett, David Duplain, John Sumner, John Miller. Front row: Austrian waiter from the Grand Hotel, Barbie Cosheril, Bob Stevenson.

The beard-growing contestants for Alderney Week 1958 at the Grand Hotel bar. Left to right: 'Chubby' Langlois, Wilfred Burland, Percy Collenette, John Bishop from 'Jean's Café', Fred 'Bibby' White, Jack Lillington, Norman Major, Andrew Herivel, Eric McVie, Sidney Simon, Sidney Carré.

Alderney Week, 1958. Miss Alderney (Ursula Jennings) with Maids of Honour, Pauline Tuckerman and Daphne Baron.

President Herivel swearing-in newly elected Francis Impey (in overcoat) as a States Member in the recently refurbished court room in January 1952. In well of court: Charles Richards (States Treasurer) and Peter Radice (Clerk of States).

Some States Members with Guernsey officials about 1969/70. Left to right: Cons. Edward Collas, Jon Kay-Mouat, John Winkworth, -?-, Eileen Sykes, Drew McQueen, Peter Radice, Dorothy Leach, Alec Forte.

St John Ambulance crew, 1957. Left to right: Sid Morris (Supt), Guida Philips (Tolley), Mrs Craven, Pauline Gaudion (Allen), Sid Simon. The ambulance was a Morris Commercial.

Alderney's 'Old Contemptibles', Remembrance Sunday, 1965. Front row, left to right: Jack Hammond, George White, 'Toby' Herivel, Charles Richards, ? Dupont.

Alderney Meat Products factory at the Arsenal, 1958. Left to right: George Beaumont, Shirley Rose, ? Tuckerman, Sadie Jennings.

Maria Osselton and Sadie Jennings potato picking, 1959.

A dinner for the over-60s about 1960. Middle row facing camera, left to right: waitresses Flo Riou and Cathy Main, Mrs Ted Odoire, Lady Sherwill, Mrs G.W. Baron, Mrs J.B. Simon, W.J. Simon, Mrs Eileen Simon, Bill Hammond.

Alderney Week float, 1965.

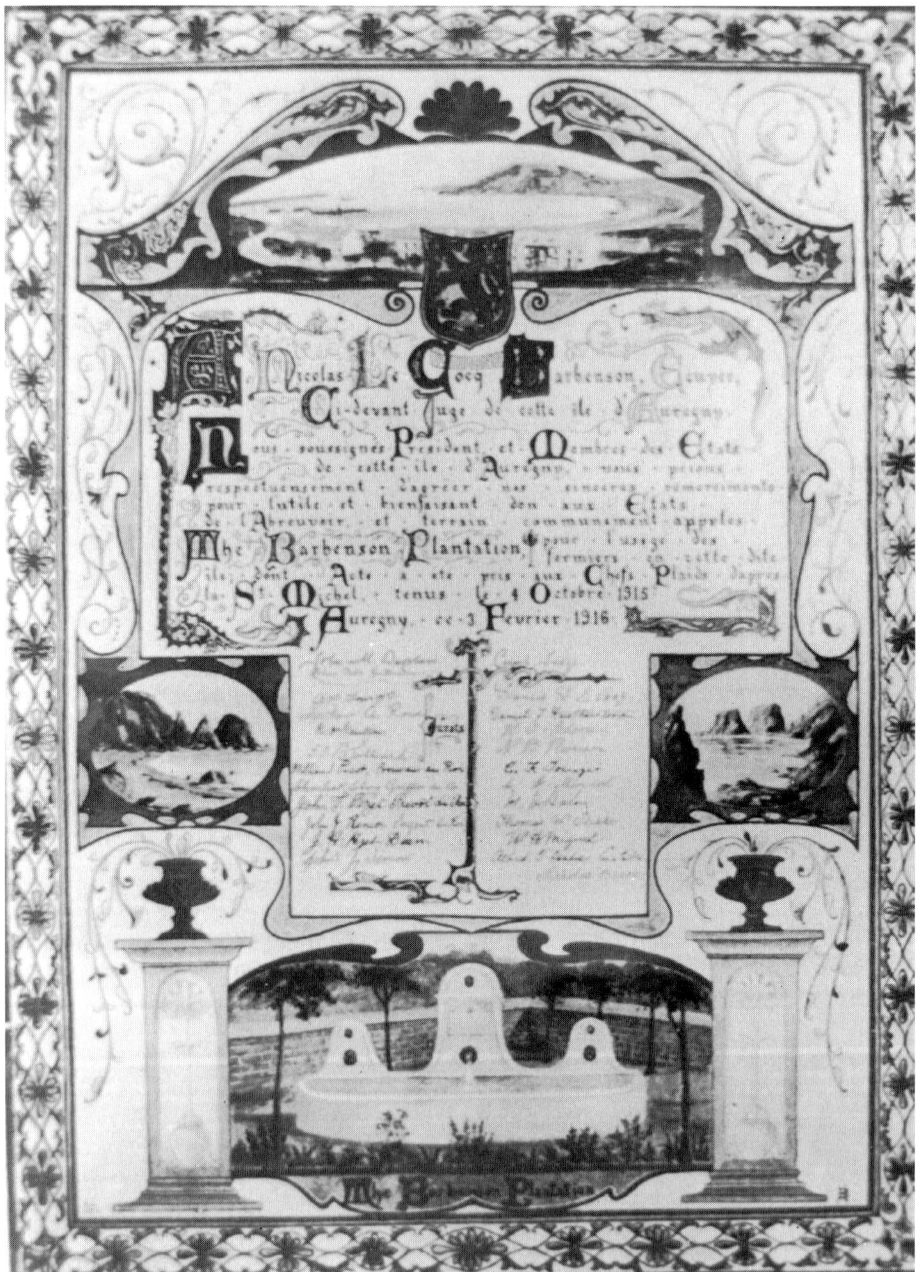

An illuminated address of thanks to Judge Barbenson from the President and Members of the States in February 1916, in return for his gift to the island of the drinking fountain, now beside the airport approach road. It was painted by Miss B. Houet. (See page 125.)

SECTION TWO

Town and Industry

Apart from cosmetic work, the main parts of St Anne are unchanged since the mid-nineteenth century, and a recently passed preservation law seeks to retain the external appearance of most of the buildings in the town centre. The oldest houses are situated in the area of Le Bourgage, the several short Venelles leading to it, Marais Square and Little Street. The better-class dwellings around Royal Connaught Square and the St Martin's area date from the more prosperous times of the late eighteenth century, with much of Victoria Street and High Street built in the mid-nineteenth century. Many of the buildings were once farmhouses with yards and cattle sheds attached to them, Alderney being from earliest times a nucleated village sited in a protective hollow, well supplied with water, and with the surrounding agricultural land farmed communally on a strip system. Even today, apart from post-war developments surrounding the edges of the town, which now join it to the later, separate, village settlements at Braye, Newtown and Crabby, there are few houses or farms outside the central area.

There was a church or at least a chapel, probably on the site of the Clock Tower, before 1050. The former church was built there by about 1300, standing with various additions, until 1851 when most of it was pulled down, after the present church had been built to accommodate the greatly increased population and the garrison. Other chapels existed on the island; one alongside the 'Nunnery' at Longis was dedicated to St Arcadrius, and is shown as La Chappelle on the map opposite the title page. The others belonged to various Frairies, a sort of medieval burial club, whose members left gifts of land or rents to the chapel for the hermit to say masses for their souls in perpetuity. These are still commemorated in a number of place names, but they were sequestered by Henry VIII at the time of the dissolution of the monasteries, and later destroyed. Their exact sites are now uncertain.

The public pumps and wells have now gone and the former gravelled streets are now tarmacked, but little else has changed in the town centre since 1945.

Alderney from the Blayes, a sketch by William le Mesurier dated 1810. He lived in a house in Royal Square (Connaught Square) opposite the vicarage, and was later the town major. Queen Victoria described him on her visit in 1854 as, 'A funny old man with a face like Punch'.

Alderney church and parsonage about 1800. Government House (now the Island Hall) is behind the trees on the left.

Scott's Hotel in Braye Road, a Westness picture from about 1890. The Belle Vue Hotel and the Methodist chapel behind it have been blanked out in printing the original postcard.

Scott's Hotel by T.A. Singleton, about 1885. The hotel and chapel can be seen clearly, and the Val stream can be seen in the Victorian brick culvert towards the bottom right.

As the plaque on the wall shows, these four cottages in Le Val were apparently also known as Simon's Place in 1904 when this picture was taken. This must have caused some confusion with the Simon's Place near Whitegates.

Royal Connaught Square in 1906. The chestnut tree planted by the Duke of Connaught the previous autumn can clearly be seen in the centre.

The Vicarage about 1870. The clergyman in the garden with his children is probably Revd le Brun.

This coloured postcard by Maureen Connolly dates from the 1930s, and shows a corner of Connaught Square.

The church covered in snow in 1895, a Westness photograph.

Interior of the parish church looking from the chancel down the nave, about 1900. This is another Westness postcard.

The Catholic church and presbytery at Crabby, about 1900.

The Methodist chapel on the left and the manse, also about 1900. The parish church is on the right.

This French pottery horseman is the sole survivor of four similar statuettes which once graced the roof ridges of Les Chevaliers in St Martin's.

An artist in Le Huret in 1965. Note the chestnut tree, planted by the Queen at the junction in 1959.

The Rink roller skating rink at the junction of High Street and Le Val in 1920. The proprietor was McClernon and the building was later used as a cinema.

Armand Toussaint at his shop on the corner of Ollivier Street in 1920.

This photo of Mrs George Simon at the pump in Le Vallée was taken by Westness about 1890.

The upper walk in The Terrace gardens, about 1900.

This lovely set of stone steps linked the upper and lower walks in The Terrace in 1900. One wonders if they are not still buried beneath the present grassy slope at this point.

Braye Road and Braye Bay, about 1900. This Westness photograph was reproduced as a postcard many times up to 1940.

Crabby village under snow in 1938.

The building of the Blue Horizon Hotel in 1936. It soon changed its name to the Grand Hotel and was the island's principal hotel until it was totally destroyed by fire in March 1981. The picture below was taken in 1952.

This .aerial view of the Grand Hotel was taken in 1938. Plans are at present being considered to rebuild it as a combined hotel/residential accommodation unit.

This photograph of the deserted High Street was taken in 1955.

The Bank of Alderney in Queen Elizabeth II Street. It flourished for a short time and failed about 1970. The resulting liquidation took some years to complete.

This photograph taken about 1946 shows the remains of the gas works at Newtown. There appears to be a wreck in the bay; if so it is probably the *Henny Fricke*.

Alderney's other source of light before the war was the small direct current electricity supply station established in this building at La Hêche in 1936.

The several sources of electricity supply installed by the Germans during the war were replaced in 1952 by this new power station built at the side of York Hill Quarry.

Two of the Blackstone generators installed in the new power station, photographed in 1954.

The Penguin Club at Newtown in 1949. It was established by the Germans as an officers' club.

The Penguin Club was destroyed by fire in 1978.

The pre-war stone crusher and associated buildings at the harbour in 1946. The island's principal employer before the war, the industry was never restarted afterwards, and the buildings were eventually demolished.

The 'Steelworks' – Cheswick and Wright's silencer factory at Newtown in 1954. The building now houses Blanchards.

A heap of silencers from the factory waiting on the quay for shipment out of the island in 1954.

Most of the good agricultural land is to be found on the high plateau area to the south and west of the town, the Grande and Petite Blayes. Traditionally this has always been unenclosed land farmed communally on the medieval strip system and surrounded by rough common land, from which it was separated by a long boundary wall of stone, earth and furze known as La Costière. Gateways on to the area were maintained on the town side. The customs associated with planting, harvest and gathering of the tithes for church and crown were strictly adhered to almost up to the Second World War. The douzaine *were responsible for seeing that the surrounding walls,* routes de souffrances *(rights of way for access to one's land) and gates were properly maintained and the land kept free of weeds. They also settled boundary disputes between neighbours. Individual plots were marked by boundary stones and over the centuries became so much divided by inheritance that some strips were only a few yards wide by 1–200 yards long. It was manured each year by large quantities of vraic, seaweed gathered from the beaches at specified times according to ancient custom, spread on the land and ploughed in, or dried, burnt as fuel in the winter and the ashes used as fertilizer. The annual banon, or communal grazing of untethered stock from two weeks after the end of harvest until the spring sowing, also helped to maintain the fertility of the soil and keep brambles and weeds down. Good crops were thus grown year after year on the same land, with little fallowing or rotation. The airport now occupies a considerable part of the best land.*

After the Second World War the agricultural base for Alderney's economy was revived for a time as a communal farm. Later, potatoes, green vegetables and flowers were exported to England, with pickers being brought from England and Guernsey when needed. The gradual reduction in frequency of sea transport caused difficulties in exporting the produce when at its best, and by the mid-1960s it had almost ceased. Today some corn is grown for cattle feed, areas of grazing maintain the two diary herds, and some potatoes are grown for local consumption, but the fields of daffodils, iris and cauliflowers are long gone.

Alderney Cow in Stable, a painting by James Ward RA, about 1860.

An Alderney cow at Watermill Farm in 1890. The picture is by Westness.

Above, another of the Watermill Farm cows in 1890; below, an Alderney bull in 1893.

Above, another view of Watermill Farm in 1893; below, cattle drinking at an '*abreuvoir publique*' on the Petite Blaye about 1900.

These sheep were photographed in the spring of 1937.

Prize-giving at the 1935 cattle show.

Rose Farm. The postmark on the original card is 21 September 1905.

Essex House in 1965. This hotel stands on the site of the early eighteenth-century home farm of the le Mesuriers. It later became the Barrackmaster's house in the 1850s and then gave its name to the lane leading down to Longis Bay.

Longis Road with Longis Villas, about 1900.

Clonque Cottage with haystack. The original from which this was copied carried the date 1856 on the back. Apart from some slight coastal erosion the scene is almost identical today.

These two Westness photographs of the Water Lanes, about 1893, show the cattle trough in Val Reuters (above, marked on the card as 'opposite Scott's Hotel') and another part of the valley with 'M.A. Lane' printed on the face of the original photograph.

Longis Common near 'The Kennels' in 1946. This herd of Jersey cows was imported by the Germans during the war. They were shipped out of the island shortly after to avoid crossing with the Guernsey breed.

Haymaking, 1946. Charlie Benfield and Bill Sebire rake up Alderney's first post-war crop.

This engraving published by Andrew & Sons about 1830 shows the Manx Sheerwater which still visits Burhou in small numbers.

This strange photograph taken on the Blayes on 5 February 1959 shows coconut matting windbreaks erected to protect the early crops in the market gardens scheme.

SECTION FOUR

Communications

The map facing the title page clearly shows the earliest jetty, at the harbour since Roman times, in Longis Bay. In 1295 Edward I awarded compensation to the people of Alderney for the damage they had suffered in one of the periodic French raids, but ten years later imposed a tax on the island to pay for repairs to the jetty which had been destroyed.

At the restoration of the monarchy in 1660 Charles II granted the island to three Jerseymen, who shortly afterwards transferred their rights to Sir George de Carteret, the King's Chamberlain. A new stone jetty was built in the 1660s, under an order from the King in 1661, after Mr George Mishaw, acting on behalf of Sir George in 1662, offered to pay £1,000 tournois towards the cost. It was completed about 1666, and in January 1674 the Alderney Court passed an ordinance decreeing a fine of 60 sous tournois on any inhabitant caught removing stones from the jetty. The remains of the old jetty can still be clearly seen today, and Longis remained the principal harbour of the island until the 'New Pier' was built at Braye in 1736.

From the building of the breakwater and Little Crabby harbour, or the 'inner harbour' starting in 1847, this pier started to silt up and was unable to cope with larger vessels. Because of the inconvenience this caused to passengers disembarking from the increasing number of vessels bringing tourists to view the construction works, after twenty-five years of argument the present commercial quay was finally built in 1898. Alderney's judge, J.A. le Cocq, who had opposed the project, resigned in consequence. The breakwater today is little more than half the length of the structure completed by 1868 when the plan to enclose the whole of Braye Bay between two huge breakwaters was finally abandoned. At certain states of the tide the 2,000 foot long line of the dismantled part, now about 20 feet below LWM, can still be clearly seen by the wave patterns it creates.

This rather grainy photograph taken about 1850 is probably the earliest surviving photo of the construction of the breakwater. It shows the gantries freshly erected each year after the winter storms to permit the lifting and placing of the huge blocks of stone for the base of the construction. These were delivered by the horse-drawn waggons seen in the centre.

Crabby and Braye between 1872 and 1874. Note the complete wall of the Fort Grosnez glacis extending right down onto Crabby beach, the RC presbytery (centre foreground), and the train of stone waggons just above it.

The breakwater workers outside Fort Grosnez in 1890, another Westness photo.

The breakwater in a storm about 1900.

This photograph of the quarry crew at Mannez with Engine No. 1 was taken about 1910. Back, left to right: Andrew Batiste, Charles Brookes (stoker), Jim Cleal (driver), Bill Quesnel, 'Drummer' Tewkesbury, Billy Oliver, Jack Enright, Wally Coombes. Front: Frank Bond, Alf Cleal, Bill Brookes, Nick Audoire, Harry Lidster, Ted Blackmore, Dick Herivel, Charlie Cleal, Mr Lihou.

Molly I in 1955. *Molly* was probably the only railway engine in the British Isles to carry a lifebelt!

The steam crane on the breakwater in 1961.

Trucks loaded at Mannez Quarry for breakwater maintenance in 1961.

Storm damage on 12 January 1962.

SS *Courier* at the slipway between 1886 and 1890. 'Casquets Jack' Houguez is leaning on the rail of the ship at the prow.

The new harbour in about 1890. Note the lime kilns on the far side, the steam launch centre foreground and the heaps of roadstone on the ground either side of the Harbour House waiting for shipment out. SS *Courier* is tied up at the quay on the right.

HMS *Mistletoe* at Braye in 1893.

Destroyers of the Channel Fleet at Braye in 1891 or 1894. Note English Row (extreme left) and the house centre foreground.

A similar scene at the 1901 manoeuvres. Note that the house in the foreground has now been enlarged and a new steam-driven stone crusher erected on Braye Common.

Special Service Vessel (tug) *Traveller*, launched in 1895 and still in service to 1920, in the foreground with Gun Vessel *Curlew*, launched in 1885, beyond. This photograph was taken in the 1901 Channel Fleet manoeuvres.

Another visit to Braye by the Channel Fleet in 1906. No. 857 is HMS *Conflict*, built in 1894, and the four-funnel destroyer in the foreground is HMS *Arab*, built in 1901.

SS *Fawn* and SS *Courier* tied up at the new jetty about 1900.

Submarine HMS *Alderney* tied up at the German jetty in 1949–50.

Motor Vessel *Island Commodore* approaching the quay in 1954.

Tanker *Shell Welder* entering the inner harbour to discharge fuel for the power station in 1957.

Trinity House Vessel *Patricia* at Braye in the 1960s.

The yacht *Riduna I* with owner Benning Arnold in the inner harbour in 1936.

A 'Sea Eagle' flying boat in trouble in a storm off the Casquets on 13 October 1923. The other landed at Braye to get help and the plane was later picked up drifting away from the Casquets and towed round to Longis Bay by the Trinity House launch *Lita*, skippered by Nick Allen with sea pilot Sam Ingrouille. They lost their punt trying to get a line to the aircraft but there were no casualties. The plane was towed round to Braye when the storm abated and flew back to Guernsey for repairs on the 15th.

Saunders-Roe 'Flying Cloud' class amphibian *Cloud of Iona* at the newly opened Alderney Airport in 1935. It had formerly landed in Braye Bay and taxied up onto the beach.

An RAF flying boat in the harbour in 1939. SS *Courier* can be seen behind, with SS *Staffa* on the right.

The first delivery of gas stoves for Duplain's shop after the war; D.H. Rapide unloading in 1947. Henry Slade and Ralph Duplain are on the right.

Alderney Airport buildings, about 1960.

De Havilland Rapide at Alderney Airport in the summer of 1954. Note the Royal Mail insignia on the tail.

The last de Havilland Rapide to visit Alderney, 1959.

A de Havilland Heron of Jersey Airlines, with Colin Bragg loading Alderney flowers for export in 1955.

Colin and Wilma Bragg (centre) with the de Havilland publicity team in 1958.

The de Havilland publicity team leaving Alderney in 1958.

Rod Taylor, the pilot of the last de Havilland Rapide to make a scheduled landing at Alderney shakes hands with air ace and King's Cup winner Tommy Rose, then manager of the Grand Hotel. Airport manager Wilma Bragg looks on.

Alderney road transport in the 1930s – a Chevrolet delivery van and a Chevrolet bus, the 'Greenhouse-on-wheels'. Left to right: W.J. Simon, Charles Dupont, Kenneth Allsop. The photograph was taken in the Butes Yard.

Riduna Bus 'To the Beach', about 1935. This Bedford bus standing in the Butes Yard was the former 'Eastern Belle'.

Alderney is about 3½ miles long by 1½ miles at its widest. The south and west coasts are characterized by almost vertical cliffs rising to nearly 300 feet and forming the southern and western boundaries of the plateau on which most of the good agricultural land is to be found. They are cut by several narrow, steep-sided valleys. From Fort Essex the ground slopes sharply down to the sand dunes of Longis Bay and Common and the flat east coast, a narrow band of land only about 20 feet above the sea. From the north-east tip of the island, apart from the rise to Fort Albert, sitting on top of Mount Touraille, sand dunes overlie the rock and continue at about 20–30 feet above sea level, all the way along the north coast to Tourgis Point where the plateau again slopes down steeply to the dune area. The whole island slopes steeply down to this narrow northern plain and the slope has several wooded valleys containing the principal streams.

Alderney is the only Channel Island with any sandstone in its geological structure, and from Clonque to Bluestone Bay almost the whole of the northern part of the island is formed of sandstone overlying the older, harder, rocks. Offshore the whole island is surrounded by small islets, large rock stacks and emergent or submerged rocks and reefs which, with the swift tides around them, constitute a considerable hazard to shipping. To the west the Nannels reef, the island of Burhou, Ortac and Les Casquets form part of a 20 mile long sandstone reef stretching almost due west from Cap de la Hague.

The cliffs and bays have always attracted photographers, and several of the oldest photographs shown here were taken by Thomas Westness who operated in Alderney from the 1880s until about 1920. His daughter continued the business in Les Rocquettes until the evacuation in 1940.

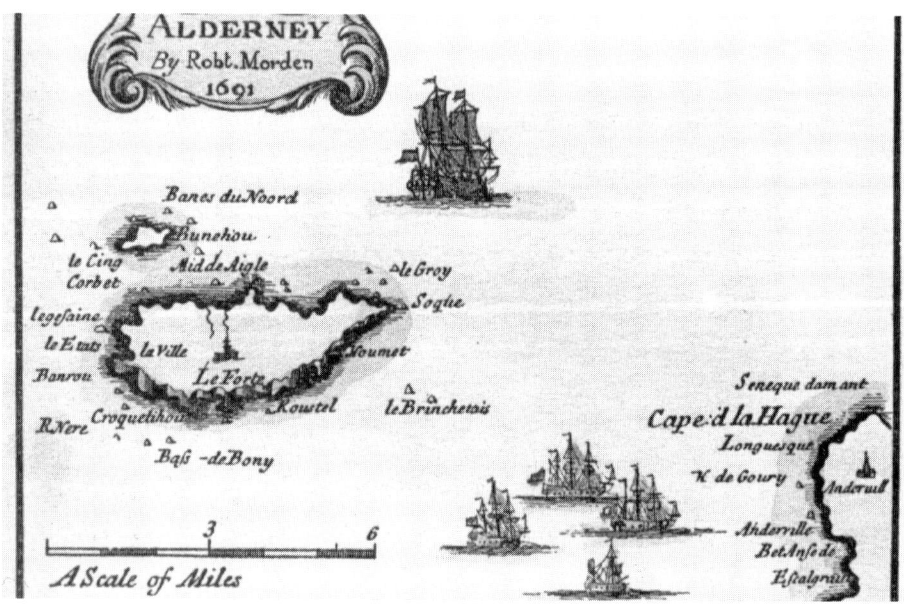

This supposedly French map of Alderney is dated 1662 but is probably a forgery as there are several inconsistencies. It shows some interesting examples of the dress of the period.

This 1691 map by Robert Mordern is one of a series of the islands off the British coasts. The scale is very inaccurate.

Above, Cachalière pier shortly after building in 1905. The automatic loading ramps shown below on a 1910 picture have yet to be built.

Longis Bay by Westness, about 1900. Fort Essex is on the hilltop with Longis Lines below.

The south-east cliffs in 1886. The Hanging Rocks are visible in the distance.

Looking the other way from the previous picture, towards the west.

The Sister Rocks from the eastern side, about 1900.

The Sister Rocks from the Telegraph Bay side in 1955.

Lion Rock at Bibette Head, about 1966.

SECTION SIX

Lighthouses and Wrecks

Tradition has always assigned to the Casquets the wreck in 1120 of La Blanche Nef *or the* White Ship *carrying Prince William, only son and heir of King Henry I, although it almost certainly happened about 25 miles away off Barfleur. There have been many other maritime tragedies around Alderney since the first written record in the parish registers in 1665, and a list of over three hundred wrecks has now been researched by the author, several of them not previously appearing in Channel Island records. Recently a wreck has been found off the north coast which appears to have been an Elizabethan warship, probably lost in 1592 but not recorded in the island. In response to the plea of many ship-owners three lighthouses were built on the Casquets Rocks and first lit in 1724, but it was not until 1912, after several shipwrecks on the rocks in front of its site, that the Alderney (also known as the Mannez or Quesnard) Lighthouse was built.*

This engraving by Jackson, taken from the *Illustrated London News* in 1868, shows the three Casquets lights with their recently heightened towers.

This earlier painting by an unknown artist shows the towers in their original form.

A 1930s brightly coloured postcard of the relief boat at the Casquets, by Maureen Connolly. The launch was the Trinity House launch *Lita*.

The Casquets by Westness. This photograph was apparently taken about 1870.

Inside the Casquets. A photo by S.C. Curtis in 1934.

This stone is to be found on Butes. It was erected for the Lloyd's signal station built there at the end of the nineteenth century. The signalman Mr Palin rested his telescope in the groove and it was then trained directly on the Casquets. Originally the left-hand side was much lower, bringing the telescope to eye level. The lower picture shows the view of the Casquets, taken from a few yards away to bypass the house recently built which now obstructs the direct view.

TBD 81 (above, left of photograph) was wrecked after striking the sunken part of the breakwater in the 1901 naval exercises. It was raised between two barges and the dockyard paddle tug *Camel* (centre), built in 1866. The lower photo shows the crew of TBD 81 on deck after the salvage operation.

TBD 81 at sea off Alderney in 1901.

SS *Burton* was wrecked on 7 January 1911. She struck the Grois reef off Château à l'Étoc, limped into harbour and sank on the rocks in the middle of Braye Bay. Her boiler and keel are still visible there at low tide.

The end of a day's outing to Burhou in 1949. The Trinity House launch *Burhou* is in the background.

This burnt-out German dredger was in the inner harbour at the end of the war.

The Alderney or Quesnard Lighthouse under construction in 1912.

The completed lighthouse in 1912, before it had been painted with its distinctive black band. Note the blacksmith's forge for Mannez Quarry on the left.

The sailing ship *Liverpool* was wrecked on Les Hommeaux Florains on 22 February 1902. This photo was taken on the 25th, by which time her sails and most of her cargo had been brought ashore.

The officers of the *Liverpool* photographed in 1898.

The Greek tanker *Constantia S* was wrecked on the Casquets on 25 January 1967, taking a cargo of drinking water to Gibraltar. In the lower picture twenty of her crew in their ship's lifeboat are about to be rescued by Trinity House Vessel *Burhou*.

TBD *Viper* at sea trial in 1899.

The wreck of TBD *Viper* on the Renonquet reef, August 1901.

The wreck of SS *Felix de Abasolo*, 7 June 1910, off Raz Island causeway.

The wreck of SS *Leros*, 29 May 1906.

The bow section of tanker *Point Law*, wrecked on 15 July 1975 at the foot of the cliffs at Puits Jervais after it had broken in two.

Motor Vessel *Armas* was wrecked on the Nannels on 26 November 1973. She broke in two some time later. The stern remained aground on the rocks and the bow section sank.

Archaeology

There are neolithic burial sites on Alderney. A few worked flint tools and arrow heads dating back as far as 150,000 years, and masses of tools from the era around 2,500 BC have been found in several sites. The burial chambers were often on elevated sites, including one occupied by the first windmill, and others where watchtowers were later built. These sites can often be identified by the local names used for the fields there, derived from the word hougue, *itself corrupted from the Norse word* haugr *meaning a mound. The only visible surviving dolmen is the small Roque Tourgie. Other sites at Longis Common and elsewhere were destroyed after the division of the common lands in 1830, and (principally) during the building of the Victorian forts. Fortunately a great deal of work was done by the Lukis family from Guernsey to excavate, investigate and preserve many of the items found then. The most significant find of this period is probably the 'Alderney Hoard' of over two hundred bronze weapons and implements, found near the site of Corblets Barracks in 1832. Similar bronze items have since been found at Raz and on Longis beach, where a wooden spear dated about 4,000 BC was found in 1983.*

Stone circles or their remains still exist on Les Rochers and at Mannez. Many Roman and earlier graves and structures were excavated near the Nunnery around the turn of the century and in the 1920s and '30s. In 1968 a bulldozer making a green for the new golf club uncovered pottery remains about 100 yards away, which on excavation revealed a late Bronze Age/early Iron Age pottery site dating from about 500 BC. Some thirty-six almost complete pots have been reconstructed, and several are on display in the Alderney Museum together with other items of the period. In the last three or four years other excavations across Longis Common up to the glacis behind Fort Albert have all tended to confirm that the earliest settlements on Alderney were in this area, before a large part of it was buried with an undated inundation of wind-blown sand, up to 2m thick, across the island from Braye to Longis.

Most recently, divers off the north-east coast have been working on what seems to be the wreck of a well-armed Elizabethan worship carrying supplies to the army in France, probably sunk in 1592. This is now under investigation.

This part of the 'Alderney Hoard' of over two hundred Bronze Age implements found on

Longis Common in 1832 is on display in the Guernsey Museum and Art Gallery.

Above, an impression of the 1745 seal of the Alderney Court from an old document. Below, an impression of the judge's seal found detached from any document; the date and provenance of this seal are unknown.

A numbered £1 note of the Alderney Commercial Bank of 1810. The bank went bankrupt after barely a year.

This is 1lb avoir of approximately 1586 with the crest of Elizabeth I and the sword mark of the City of London. It was recovered from the Elizabethan wreck recently found off Alderney.

Some of the early Iron Age pottery found at Les Huguettes site in 1966, now on view in the Alderney Museum.

Two views of a Bronze Age socketed axe head found on Longis beach.

Rocque Tourgie, or Roc à L'Épine, the Neolithic dolmen near Fort Tourgis.

A recent view of the 'Lavoiret' or washing place at Ladysmith. This was one of three places where the island women did their washing in former times.

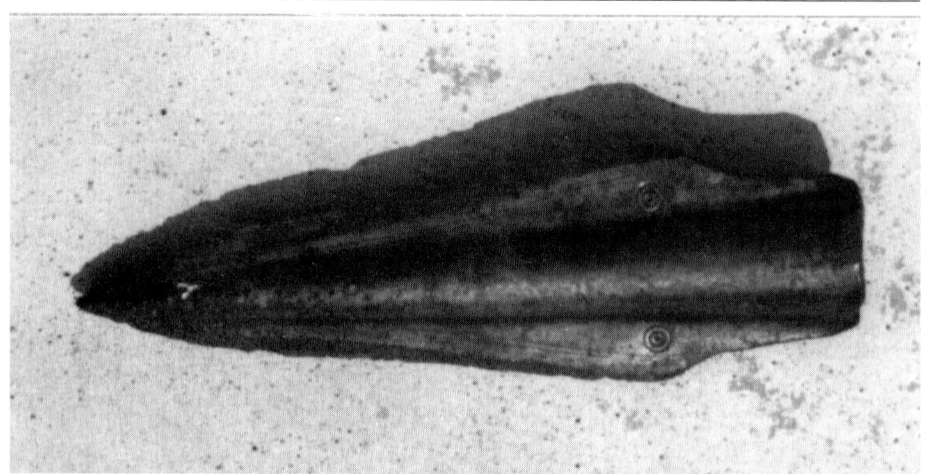

A Bronze Age socketed spearhead found at Longis.

A Neolithic stone hammer found in Alderney in the 1830s.

'Blue Bridge', built by the Victorians to carry the road to Fort Clonque over the stream at Vau Pommiers. A severe storm in April 1991 eroded the cliff face and exposed the much older stone 'souk' below it.

The two sides of a bronze Roman sestertius dated AD 78 or 79, found below the eroded cliff at Hannaine Bay.

Top left: the remains of the vraic road at Longis. Right: the Admiralty crest on the 1906 pumps at Coastguards. Below left: one of the four boundary stones to the Victorian pumping station on the Petite Blaye supplying Fort Tourgis. Right: the pump was converted to electricity after the war; it has long been disused.

Military Alderney

The 'Nunnery' at Longis Bay has its origins in a Roman fort built to protect the safe anchorage in the bay. Rebuilt or strengthened in the fourteenth and fifteenth centuries, and still retaining much of its medieval stonework, it owes its present form with the covered gateway on the eastern side to a programme of fortifications against Napoleon in 1793. The only surviving sixteenth-century fortification is Essex Castle, the remaining part of the outer walls of which dominate the hill above the Nunnery. This was built with a strong inner keep between 1546 and 1563. The 'pepperpot' lookout was added about 1815. The keep and part of the walls were demolished in the 1850s to make way for the present Fort Essex, built as a military hospital.

The building of the 'Harbour of Refuge' a thinly disguised term for a naval base, at Braye from 1847 created a need to defend the harbour, and a chain of forts and batteries was therefore built all round the island, most of them obliterating former defence works and watchtowers on the same sites.

The militia, which had for centuries consisted of almost all able-bodied men between sixteen and sixty-five, was at its most active from the time of the governorship of Alderney by the le Mesurier family, and the first proper uniform was issued in 1781. The infantry and artillery sections had a small unit of light dragoons with a sergeant and twelve troopers added for a few years around the turn of the nineteenth century. At this time the Alderney force had a complement 19 officers, 20 sergeants, 7 drummers and 339 men. The Channel Island militias were granted the title 'royal' in 1831, and with the erection of the forts and the enormous increase in the regular army garrisons from 1854, the Royal Alderney Militia became an all artillery force, with responsibilities as a coastal defence unit. In 1905 it was turned into a volunteer force of 100 men in peacetime and 180 men during a war.

Despite the traditional exemption for Channel islanders from military service outside the islands, a large part of the militia volunteered for service in the First World War and forty-one men from the island lost their lives in the conflict. The garrison was finally withdrawn and the militia disbanded in 1929. Twenty-four more died in the Second World War.

Fort Corblets, about 1930.

Fort Clonque, a Westness photograph from about 1900.

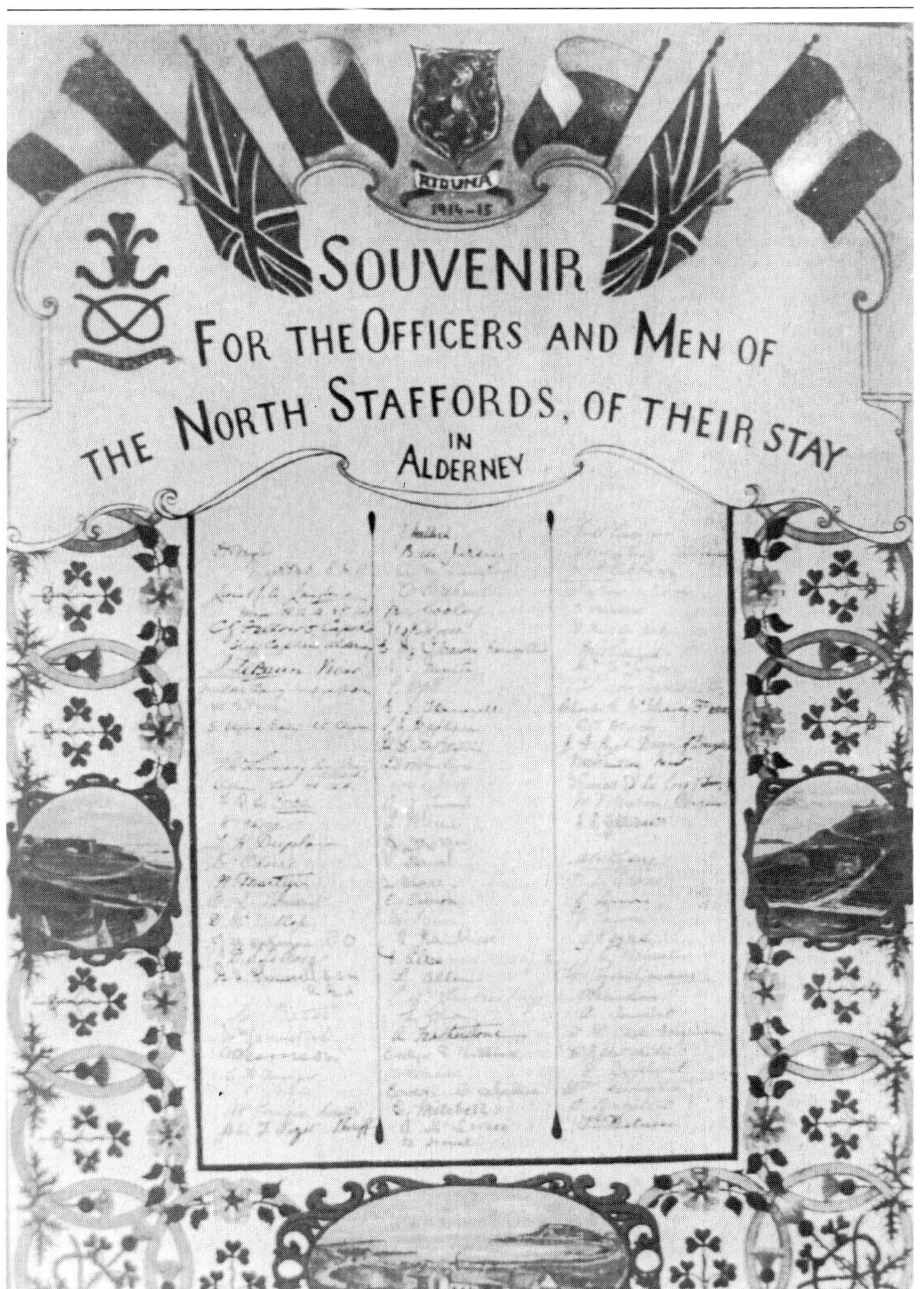

An illuminated address given by the states and people of Alderney to the 1914–15 garrison on their departure to the First World War. The address was penned by Miss B. Houet, the adopted daughter of photographer Westness. She later became Mrs Harper and was quite well known in England as a watercolour artist.

The men of the Alderney Militia volunteered en masse for service in the First World War. Two contingents left the island on SS *Courier* on 20 and 27 March 1915 to join the Guernsey contingent for training.

Garrisoning Alderney's island forts must have been pretty uncomfortable, even when they were new. These two recent pictures show Fort Houmet Herbé (above) and Fort Les Hommeaux Florains (below) at high tide in rough weather.

Above, the Nunnery, Fort Essex, and Longis Lines, about 1900. Note 'frying pan' battery at the left end of the low cliff with the flag flying. Below, a similar view drawn by I.T. Carey in 1810, before Essex Castle was partly demolished to build the fort, and before the batteries were built. The barracks in the centre were built about 1793. Note the watchtower on top of the hill above the Hanging Rocks. The rocks in the foreground by the picnickers are the standing stones of Les Porciaux Dolmen.

Essex Barn with no roof, the old canteen and the barrack block, about 1900.

Fort Tourgis, about 1890.

The Royal Alderney Artillery and Engineer Militia parading just inside Fort Grosnez in 1907. By this time the militia was a smaller volunteer force. In the picture are Nick Buckland (second from left), Tom Simon (second from right), William Sebire (fifth from right), John Godfray, and John Le Gros (marked X).

NCOs and men of the 'Alderney Siege Contingent' in training at Bexhill in 1916. I have been unable to identify individuals.

An engraved bronze medallion about 6 inches across like this one was awarded to the families of men killed in the First World War. Alfred George from Alderney was killed in 1916. His medallion and campaign medals can be seen in the Alderney Museum.

Recruits of G Company, the 341st Machine Gun Battalion, in training in Alderney in 1940.

The coastguard look-out on Essex Hill, built in 1906. The building was also used as a look-out by the Germans during the Second World War, but was later demolished. The railings and the brick floor of the octagonal look-out point can still be seen there.

The Arsenal, drawn by Louisa Lane Clarke in 1851.

The Occupation

Almost the entire population of the island was evacuated on 23 June 1940 ahead of Hitler's advance across Europe, leaving behind all of their animals and most of their possessions. In the following ten days or so, before the Germans arrived in the island on 2 July, parties from Guernsey removed most of the animals, much of the stock of the shops, and the drugs and equipment from the hospital. Some looting of private houses also occurred. The airfield was obstructed with barbed wire and abandoned lorries. The first German units to arrive were anti-aircraft and spotter units, and the island was only lightly defended, with a sergeant major in charge. About three weeks later the Germans in Guernsey sent over other civilian parties to remove useful equipment, harness, fodder and stores, and to harvest the potato crop. This was supposed to take about three weeks but in the end the party stayed nearly two years, growing corn and potatoes intended to feed the German garrison in Guernsey.

By June 1941 the garrison was about 450 men. More troops were moved in, using the abandoned houses and forts as quarters. To provide labour for the erection of more defences, paid volunteer Organisation Todt (OT) workers were drafted in from Europe to erect camps of sectional buildings, an electricity system and other necessary facilities. In October 1941, having given up his immediate plans to invade England, Hitler issued orders to fortify the Channel Islands as part of his Atlantic wall defences from Norway to the Spanish border. Four camps were put up, two at Platte Saline and Saye Bay, each for about 1,500 slave-workers, who arrived from August 1942, many of them from eastern Europe. A third near the Catholic cemetery housed up to 1,000 German and paid OT technicians. The fourth at L'Emauve south of the airport could house about 1,000, but was converted in February 1943 into a concentration camp for prisoners forming a construction brigade from Neuengamme Concentration Camp in Germany, with a unit of SS guards. By this time there were about 2,500 troops in the island plus the OT workers. By May 1943, with the construction of defence works well under way the garrison was 3,800 troops and there were up to 5,000 slave-workers living under appalling conditions, poorly fed and clothed, frequently beaten and with no medical care. There were still 3,200 troops here in September 1944, and after D-Day the SS unit and many of the surviving slaves were taken back to Europe. Supplies of food, cement and steel reinforcing were short and the construction work was greatly curtailed.

Most of the pictures in this section have come from members of the garrison, then mostly young soldiers or naval ratings, who have revisited Alderney in recent years.

These unique photographs were enlarged from a short length of 9.5mm cine film shot by a German Propaganda Ministry photographer in 1942. They show an Organisation Todt overseer and OT slave workers digging a deep trench in Val Fontaine, behind Longis Villas.

German anti-aircraft battery look-out post in the old coastguard post on Essex Hill in 1942.

An aerial view of the remains of Sylt Concentration Camp the day before the island was liberated in 1945. The trenches dug across the airfield to prevent landings are similar to today's pattern of runways.

The rangefinder on top of the fire-control tower at Mannez (the 'Odeon') in May 1945 when the island was freed.

Civil Affairs administrator Sonder-führer Hans Herzog (left) with Lt Berheim-Erft standing on the quay by the minesweeper which took them to Jersey when they left the island on 10 April 1942.

German officers and men with the flock of sheep brought in to feed the garrison, at an Alderney farm around 1942–3.

Cattle grazing on the wired-off slopes of Fort Tourgis in July 1941.

A German 260mm shell in a frame adapted as an anti-tank bomb trap, exposed on Corblets beach after a violent storm from 2 to 5 January 1960.

German cooks at their dugout shelter in
Hauteville in 1942.

Braye Road and Newtown from York Hill
in 1943. Note the camouflaged hut.

A German hut by Longis Villas in 1943. The base is still there.

Light railways and slave workers at Fort Albert in 1943.

SECTION TEN
Post-War Alderney

The Germans in Jersey and Guernsey surrendered on 9 May 1945, but Alderney was not relieved until the 16th, when Force 135 under Brigadier Alfred Snow steamed into Braye Harbour and the German Commander, Colonel Schwalm, surrendered without a shot being fired. They found the island devastated; most of the buildings at Braye and Crabby and a number of those in town had no roofs, floors or windows, the wood having been burnt for fuel. Some had been demolished altogether to provide a clear field of fire. The parish and Catholic churches had been turned into stores. There was rubbish and rubble everywhere, as well as barbed wire and minefields totalling over 37,000 mines. There were nearly 400 marked graves of the prisoners, in the churchyard and on Longis Common, and 61 graves of Germans at a cemetery next to the Stranger's Cemetery.

About 2,500 German troops were shipped to England the next day as prisoners-of-war and the remainder were put to work removing the mines and booby traps and clearing up the rubble. The Army engineers and a team of Ministry of Works building workers set about repairing the breakwater and some of the houses, and later erected new houses to replace those demolished. Small groups of islanders led by Judge French came to assess the situation, and after various negotiations the islanders began to return in December 1945. A communal farm was set up; the first harvest in 1946, made difficult by wet weather, was followed by a harsh winter. A Home Office committee of enquiry was set up to determine the future status and government of Alderney. The troops were withdrawn in August 1946, and the communal farm was disbanded at the end of 1947, after which the island was on its own. Judge French also resigned at the end of 1947 and a new judge was appointed until the new constitution was agreed. The major pre-war employer, the granite works, never restarted, agriculture was soon to become much reduced in scale, and progress was slow. More than half of the pre-war population had returned by then and new settlers began to arrive. In 1948 the pre-war sporting activities were resumed and the Alderney Week festival and cattle show was held.

The present administrative system of the island was set up under a new law which came into force on 1 January 1949 when elections were held, for the first time by universal suffrage, for the nine states members and the new office of president. Jurats in future were to be appointed by the Home Office. By 1961 the population was back to its pre-war figure and tourists were coming in increasing numbers. The new settlers, many of them retired ex-colonial civil servants and administrators, brought a degree of prosperity with their need for new houses and their contributions to taxes. Alderney has had some hard times since but has always remained totally self supporting financially, despite the necessity of providing services in line with those available in the UK and Guernsey.

Clearing up the mess and remaking the road in Carrière Viront in 1946.

Laying the first tarmacked surface on the dirt road at La Marette, about 1960.

The devastated warehouses in Braye Street and a camouflaged 47mm anti-tank gun casemate on the beach in 1945.

German electricity pylons near Whitegates and the concrete sleepers brought to relay the railway line to Mannez Quarry in 1950.

The inner harbour in 1950/1. The German crane was still in use.

The new power station in course of erection in 1952.

Three Ruston horizontal two-cylinder engines, driving the generators in the power station in April 1953.

A rare view of the old quarry buildings in Battery Quarry in 1951. These are about 100 feet down and usually under at least 60 feet of water.

Fort Corblets with Château à L'Étoc beyond, about 1948, when Francis Impey's market garden scheme was in full swing in the middle of the picture.

Charlie Mignot with the island's first set of twin Guernsey calves in 1946.

Steam engine *Molly I* with trucks of stone for breakwater repairs in 1965.

Slightly out of place here, this Hillman taxi outside the Marais Hall was decorated for the coronation of King George V in 1937.

Mannez Quarry and the 'Odeon' in June 1955. Note the fallen 2cm AA-gun bunker which had been undercut by quarrying activity.

The Alderney Library was in this house in High Street in 1954.

The fortieth anniversary of the return of the 'Boat People' to Alderney after the war was celebrated by the minting of this bronze lapel badge the size of a shilling, still worn with pride by those islanders who returned in 1945.

The fiftieth anniversary of the evacuation was celebrated by the unveiling of a plaque at Weymouth harbour (the port at which the evacuees arrived in 1940) by the Mayor of Weymouth. This pottery plate was presented to the island to mark the occasion.

Royal Visits

Since King John lost his possessions in France in 1204, the Channel Islands have remained the personal possessions of the sovereign who still retains the title of Duke of Normandy, and the loyal toast in the islands is 'To the Queen, our Duke'. The first sovereign known to have visited Alderney was Queen Victoria in 1854. Since the Second World War several members of the royal family have been welcomed, starting with Princess Elizabeth in 1949. Since becoming queen in 1952, Her Majesty has made four visits, the most recent of which, although not an old photograph, is illustrated on the last page of this volume.

This banner, 'THE KEY TO THE CHANNEL WELCOMES YOU', was erected at the top of the breakwater slipway for the arrival of the Duke of Connaught in September 1905. The photo of the arrival was later put out as a postcard, printed the wrong way round so that the message could be easily read.

Princess Elizabeth visiting the Valley Gardens scheme in 1949. Left to right: Lt Governor of Guernsey, HRH the Princess Elizabeth, Francis Impey (owner of the gardens), President of Alderney, Cdr 'Toby' Herivel.

The Princess talks to the children in 1949. Public school children are in the foreground, with Convent School pupils on the right.

The Princess inspecting the British Legion members. Left to right: Bill Dunne, -?-, Cecil Coysh, Mrs Johnson, Mrs Lilian Coe, -?-, -?-, George Gaudion, Princess Elizabeth, Peirson Sumner, Lt Governor, Cdr Herivel.

HM The Queen laying the foundation stone for the new Mignot Memorial Hospital at Crabby, 27 July 1957. Watching are Mabel Marriette, Mrs Herivel (in pale suit), and Fred Marriette. Cdr Herivel is beside Her Majesty, and Tommy Rose is behind her.

The Queen talks to the guides and brownies on her 1957 visit.

The Duke of Edinburgh inspects the British Legion on this same visit. Left to right: Charles Richards, Phyllis Richards, Brigadier Cosby, -?-, the Duke, -?-, -?-, Victor Coysh, John Carré, Bobby Allen, Mrs Laverty, -?-.

Princess Margaret pays Alderney a visit on 24 June 1959.

The Queen Mother visited on 12 May 1963 and stayed overnight.

The Queen Mother was met at the airport with a bouquet. On her right Lt Governor Vice-Admiral Sir Geoffrey Robson, on her left Cdr and Mrs Herivel.

Inspecting the Legion on the slipway. Left to right: Major Bob Sivers, the Queen Mother, Hank Lawrence, Mrs Laverty, Colin Bragg, Wilma Bragg, -?-, -?-.

Another visit from the Queen Mother on 29 May 1975 to open the new extension to the Alderney Society Museum.

HM The Queen came again on 29 June 1978. Left to right: HM The Queen, Olive Hammond, Eileen Simon, Sid Simon, Edna Bichard, Charles Bichard.

The Queen leaving the Island Hall after a Vin d'Honneur on 24 May 1989.

The royal yacht *Britannia* dressed over-all, with the royal barge taking Her Majesty back to the ship on her departure.

Acknowledgements

As in the first volume, family photographs, postcards, paintings and engravings have been generously loaned by many people and organizations both on and off the island. Grateful thanks go to all of them for the opportunity to examine and copy them, and for permission to reproduce them here. Once again, in some instances, the same item came from several different sources and the best reproduction has been selected for this volume.

A few photographs are recent pictures by the author to show old structures or items of which there appears to be no other suitable record, and a number are from his own collection of original prints, maps and postcards. For the rest he has to thank:

The States of Alderney; the States of Guernsey; the Priaulx Library in Guernsey; the Alderney Society; Alderney Electricity Ltd; the Alderney Library; the *Alderney Journal* and the Institution of Civil Engineers. All graciously allowed items from their collections to be copied.

Individuals who have contributed items to this selection include the following:

Colin Benfield • Colin and Wilma Bragg • May Brennan • Julian Chatte Victor Coysh • Mr and Mrs Cranwell • David Duplain • Vi Dupont • Andrew Eggleston • the late A.H. Ewen • Iris and Dan Godfray • Richard Heaume Eileen Hoskins • Major A. Hynes • Fred Jennings • Richard Lamerton Graham Lawson • Charles McDonald • the late Alastair Alpin McGregor • Bryan Mauger • Jean Mellish • Group Captain E.F.L. Odoire • the late Peter Radice K.R. Rawlings • Bill Rowe • Sid Simon • Frank Smith • Eileen Sykes • Carel Toms • Alec Tucker • Jack Quinain • Thora Walker • the late Leslie Wells Douglas Whitworth.